The
Land
Jesus Knew

The Land Jesus Knew

eagle

Guildford, Surrey

Copyright © 2001 Eagle Publishing

British Library Cataloguing in Publication Data.
A catalogue record for this book is available from the
British Library.

Published by Eagle Publishing PO Box 530, Guildford,
Surrey GU2 4FH.

Typeset by Eagle
Printed in Hong Kong
ISBN No: **0 86347 458 6**

Dedication

To the countless pilgrims and visitors to the Holy
Land throughout the ages who have visited the sites
mentioned in the footsteps of their Lord.

Polish Jews waiting to embark at Jaffa having visited
the Holy Land, 1839.

TABLE OF CONTENTS

INTRODUCTION

In the 2,000 years or so since Jesus lived and walked in the land of Israel there have been many radical changes both to the land and to the people. Never has there been so much change as in the twentieth century. The Middle East has seen a dramatic increase in population, partially due simply to increased life expectancy and healthier living conditions amongst the indigenous inhabitants. But the main reason for growth has been, and continues to be, the influx of Jews returning to their land.

The Zionist movement started slowly last century when Jews already had lived in Israel for centuries amongst the Arab and Palestinian populations. They were, however, never masters in their land, which had been successively under the influence of various Arab princes, subject to the repeated and often bloody conquests of the Crusaders, a vassal to the Ottoman Empire, and subject to countless attacks and counter—attacks, the scene of power plays during the nineteenth and early part of the twentieth century. The Zionist movement since the end of the nineteenth century, encouraged the immigration of

Jews who settled the land, portions of which were sparsely populated. During the 1930s and early 1940s the Jewish Resistance movement became more and more vocal, culminating in the creation of the modern State of Israel in 1948. By this time, the world had been outraged by the holocaust and the treatment Jews had suffered, principally in countries under Nazi rule. The time was ripe for the official declaration of independance and for the acknowledgement of support by the West for the

State of Israel in diplomatic, financial and military terms.

In the wake of this declaration a number of things happened that would force the pace of change in the land — and would in some places radically transform the land beyond recognition. The Arab and Palestinian populations were, on the whole, separated

The Walls of the Old Jerusalem, by Carl Werner

from the Jewish population both through the ensuing wars (1947—49, 1956, 1967, 1973), through the creation of refugee camps, and through the ever-

The walls of Jerusalem with the Citadel in the background

increasing numbers of Jews returning to Israel. Some of these returnees arrived dramatically, such as the first boat loads at the end of the Second World War, or those Jews from Ethiopia airlifted in 1984 and 1991. Other arrived and continue to arrive in less dramatic ways, including those re-settling today from the former Soviet Union.

This huge population increase — there are now 6 million people in the land compared to around 500,000 at the turn of the century — has resulted in the creation of the large city of Tel Aviv, the dramatic expansion of Jerusalem and the Palestinian towns and camps in the Gaza strip. The countryside has changed beyond recognition with huge irrigation programmes diverting water from the Sea of Galilee. This has resulted in fertile, irrigated areas not only in the north and centre of the country, but even in the south, where the desert can truly be said to be flowering. Other changes have been to the infra-structure of the country, with the creation of roads, motorways, electricity generation, military camps and archeological digs.

This dramatic change is all the more obvious when comparing specific sites with descriptions by earlier travellers and by consulting earlier pictorial records. These exist in the form of photographs, from the 1860s on and, although their quality is often uneven, photographs from the twentieth century abound, either in black and white or in colour, particularly since the 1950s.

However, the earliest visual records are those by various artists although virtually nothing exists before 1800, and the early material was often sketchy and inexact in its rendition of the main sites. Most of the early artistic endeavours focused on the holy sites: the churches and shrines of Christianity, particularly in Jerusalem, and hold little interest for the contemporary reader.

In many ways David Roberts picked up on this centuries-old interest when he visited the Holy Land — just as many pilgrims had before him. David Roberts, however, was principally interested in documenting the sites of religious and geographic interest. This book is based upon his work carried out during his momentous journey of 1839 to 1840. Roberts, who was of Scottish origin, was an excellent draughtsman and a accomplished painter in water-colours. He had already executed numerous scenes throughout the British Isles and undertaken one

*The centre of Bethlehem today with churches and mosques in
close proximity.*

overseas trip to Spain focusing on the Moorish architecture of Seville and the south. Having arrived from Egypt, David Roberts was to spend over one year criss-crossing the land from southern Lebanon to Jordan and the Sinai peninsular. Upon his return to England, over 250 large-format watercolours had been completed, each measuring approximately 90 x 60 cm. Over the next six years Louis Haghe, a Belgian platemaker and master engraver working in London, prepared 250 of these for reproduction in

lithograph form. These were carefully printed and hand coloured. A limited edition of 500 copies was produced, luxuriously bound variously in three to six volumes and printed by Francis Graham Moon. The sale was by subscription and by the time the last volume was completed all had been sold to the great of the land, from Queen Victoria and the Prime Minister, countless aristocrats and collectors.

In the following years numerous other editions were printed in order to satisfy public demand. A few were of the original format; most were smaller. But in all cases the quality of the first numbered edition was never matched. All David Roberts reproductions in this book have been reproduced from the original edition, a copy of which is kept in the British Library.

David Roberts work was seminal in many ways. He was extremely exact in his representation of buildings and archaeological remains. In the manner of his execution there was no room for exaggeration or invention when it came to the depiction of specific locations. This can be seen when comparing his views of Jerusalem (on pages 98 to 101 in particular) with photographs of the same site today. Roberts is therefore a thoroughly reliable witness.

However, the artist did allow himself some licence, evident in the foreshortening of hills and other features far in the distance. Even here, we must remember that there was far less atmospheric pollution in his day, and that many other European artists, when visiting the Holy Land, commented on the extreme clarity of the atmosphere. A comparison of photographs of the Dead Sea (pages 106 to 109) or the Sea of Galilee (pages 62 to 64) will demonstrate this. Even here, though, Roberts was careful to ensure that he was not inventing mountains, but simply showing them in their true form, though rather more clearly and dramatically than in reality.

Roberts also portrayed the inhabitants he met, whether a group of men sitting and talking in front of the Pool of Bethesda in Jerusalem (pages 74 and 75), an encampment of pilgrims near Jericho (pages 50 to 51) or a group of travellers on their way up from the shores of the Sea of Galilee (pages 94). From these we have a good idea of their dress and habits, which seem very foreign to a late twentieth-century Western eye.

When visiting the Holy Land, David Roberts kept

Jerusalem, with the flooded Pool of Bethesda, by Nathaniel Green

a detailed diary in which he described the people he met and the places he visited. Extracts from his diaries will be found throughout this book along with comments describing some of the sites today. His illustrations and descriptions are complemented by Jon Arnold s photography of the same sites today. A professional photographer, Jon visited Israel twice in

1995 to track down and photograph the sites recorded over 150 years earlier. These photographs throw a new light on the land and the many changes it has undergone, particularly in the last fifty years.

Most importantly, however, the reader will find selected biblical passages. *The Land Jesus Knew* only really makes sense when photographs and water-colours serve to document the places that Jesus knew and the events that took place there. By attempting to give a feel for the land we hope that the events and teaching will be all the more grounded and relevant to the reader once the Gospel text has reminded us of Jesus words and the significant events in his life. It is

all too easy to see Jesus outside the geographical context in which he lived and so to apply his words exclusively to our situation today, when they can be seen to have a universal application throughout the centuries and from culture to culture.

David Wavre
Guildford
October 2000

Chapter 1

The Angel Appears to Mary

The Gospels record of the life of Jesus starts with two different aspects of the foretelling of his birth. One consists of the genealogies found in Matthew and Luke, establishing Jesus lineage and the fact that he was the long-heralded Messiah, born from David s line. The other consists of the annunciation in which the angel Gabriel visits Mary, a young Jewish girl, promised in marriage to Joseph, to announce that she has been chosen by God to bear his Son, the Saviour of the world. The Gospels document that Mary lived at that time in Nazareth, but not where in Nazareth. And here we immediately hit the first major problem that has exercised pilgrims and churchmen alike over the centuries. The exact locations of some of the events were never recorded. Indeed, they seemed unimportant to the writers of the Gospels and to the early Christians.

This fascination with identifying precise locations can be traced back to the early fourth century and to Helena, the mother of the Emperor Constantine, in particular. Around the year AD325, she toured the Holy Land comprehensively in the wake of her son s conversion and subsequent declaration that Christianity was to become the official religion of the Roman Empire. Her visit was associated with a large and lavish programme of church building, in particular in Jerusalem, but also throughout the land. It must be remembered that from the destruction of the temple in AD 70 until then, Jerusalem was an

Nazareth: St Gabriel, the Greek Orthodox Church of the Annunciation.

insignificant town, specifically deprived of all rights under the heavy-handed retribution for the attempted revolt against Roman rule.

The emperor, following his conversion to Christianity some twenty years earlier, took an intense personal interest in his mother s church building programme which he lavishly funded. He wrote to the bishop of Jerusalem on matters of design and furnishing, promising financial and administrative help, along with transportation facilities and other assistance to the building programme.

Helena had been busy identifying sites throughout the Holy Land relating to the annunciation, the birth of Jesus, the preaching of the beatitudes and the

A general view of Nazareth in 1851, by Van de Velde.

ascension, along with sites in Jerusalem relating to the events of Holy Week: the site of the upper room, Pilate s court, the high priest s house, the Via Dolorosa and the site of the crucifixion.

And so, while the exact geographical location of the town of Nazareth has never been in doubt, considerable caution must be exercised before identifying any specific site in the town as the precise location of the actual annunciation. The Church of the Annunciation has been built above one supposed site, a grotto hollowed into the ground and called the Shrine of the Annunciation, while another site, the Fountain of the Virgin, is held to be the exact location by others. Such controversies are unlikely to be resolved.

According to Roberts, the most popularly honoured of all relics in Nazareth is a stone named the table of our Lord . This is a large flat slab of common local sandstone at which Jesus is supposed to have dined.

There is not an object in Nazareth so much the resort of pilgrims, Greek, Romish, Arab, and even Turk, as this stone. The Greek and Latin pilgrims resorting to it from devotion, and the Arab and the Turk to see the wonders which it is presumed to work on the devotees.

The chapel has been substantially remodelled, as can be seen from comparing David Robert s view of the Chapel of the Annunciation with the modern photograph. The original church, added to over the centuries, has been stripped away to reveal, far more clearly, the original stone table and the remains of the earliest construction. This reconstruction enables us to better appreciate the original, but also better accommodates the ever-increasing number of visitors and pilgrims.

23

The interior of the Church of the Annunciation, by David Roberts

A service in progress in the Church of the Annunciation today. The alcove in the centre behind the altar is the shrine of the Annunciation.

Let us look now at the simple and moving Gospel account:

In the sixth month, God sent the angel Gabriel to Nazareth, a town in Galilee, to a virgin pledged to be married to a man named Joseph, a descendant of David.

The virgin's name was Mary. The angel went to her and said, 'Greetings, you who are highly favoured! The Lord is with you.'

Mary was greatly troubled at his words and wondered what kind of greeting this might be. But the angel said to her, 'Do not be afraid, Mary, you have found favour with God. You will be with child and give birth to a son, and you are to give him the name Jesus. He will be great, and will be called the Son of the Most High. The Lord God will give him the throne of his father David, and he will reign over the house of Jacob for ever; his kingdom will never end.'

'How will this be,' Mary asked the angel, 'since I am a virgin?'

The angel answered, 'The Holy Spirit will come upon you, and the power of the Most High will overshadow you. So the holy one to be born will be called the Son of God. Even Elizabeth your relative is going to have a child in her old age, and she who was said to be barren is in her sixth month. For nothing is impossible with God.'

'I am the Lord's servant,' Mary answered. 'May it be to me as you have said.' Then the angel left her.

(Luke 1:26–38)

Chapter 2

The Birth of Jesus

After Jesus was born in Bethlehem in Judea, during the time of King Herod, Magi from the east came to Jerusalem and asked, 'Where is the one who has been born king of the Jews? We saw his star in the east and have come to worship him.'

When King Herod heard this he was disturbed, and all Jerusalem with him. When he had called together all the people's chief priests and teachers of the law, he asked them where the Christ was to be born. 'In Bethlehem in Judea,' they replied, 'for this is what the prophet has written:

'But you, Bethlehem, in the land of Judah,
 are by no means least among the rulers of Judah;
for out of you will come a ruler
 who will be the shepherd of my people Israel." '

Then Herod called the Magi secretly and found out
from them the exact time the star had appeared. He sent
them to Bethlehem and said, 'Go and make a careful
search for the child. As soon as you find him, report to me,
so that I too may go and worship him.'

After they had heard the king, they went on their way,

and the star they had seen in the east went ahead of them until it stopped over the place where the child was. When they saw the star, they were overjoyed. On coming to the house, they saw the child with his mother Mary, and they bowed down and worshipped him. Then they opened their treasures and presented him with gifts of gold and of incense and of myrrh. And having been warned in a dream not to go back to Herod, they returned to their country by another route.

(Matthew 2:1–12)

Bethlehem today has changed beyond recognition from the sleepy little town it was 150 years ago. The prime site of Manger Square is in the foreground with the Church of the Nativity to the right.

In every age of Christianity Bethlehem has held a special place in the hearts of believers as the site of the birth of Jesus. Furthermore, the place of the nativity was distinctly foretold in prophecy. The Gospel text below relating this event is familiar to all today.

The town has grown since then, and indeed very substantially since David Roberts visit. He comments little on Bethlehem itself, simply stating:

> *The village lies about two hours distance from Jerusalem, on the east and north-east slope of a long ridge; a deep valley, Wady Taamirah, being on the south side, which passes into the Dead Sea.*
>
> *The surrounding country, though hilly, is fertile and well cultivated. In the distance are seen the hills of Moab, and below them is a glimpse of the Dead Sea.*

The surrounding hillside is still today reasonably fertile and cultivated. Sheep still graze on some of the hillsides which appear to have changed little from that night when the shepherds watched over their original flocks.

> *And there were shepherds living out in the fields near by, keeping watch over their flocks at night. An angel of the Lord appeared to them, and the glory of the Lord shone around them, and they were terrified. But the angel said to them, 'Do not be afraid. I bring you good news of great joy that will be for all the people. Today in the town of David a Saviour has been born to you; he is Christ the Lord. This will be a sign to you: You will find a baby wrapped in cloths and lying in a manger.'*
>
> *Suddenly a great company of the heavenly host appeared with the angel, praising God and saying,*
>
> *'Glory to God in the highest,*
> *and on earth peace to men on whom his favour rests.'*

When the angels had left them and gone into heaven, the shepherds said to one another, 'Let's go to Bethlehem and see this thing that has happened, which the Lord has told us about.'

So they hurried off and found Mary and Joseph, and the baby, who was lying in the manger. When they had seen him, they spread the word concerning what had been told them about this child, and all who heard it were amazed at what the shepherds said to them. But Mary treasured up all these things and pondered them in her heart. The shepherds returned, glorifying and praising God for all the things they had heard and seen, which were just as they had been told.

(Luke 2:8–20)

The Shepherds' fields today

Chapter 3

The Flight Into Egypt

Rolling hills, small villages and broad vistas characterise the countryside around Hebron today, though the town itself is a large Palestinian urban sprawl.

When [the Magi] had gone, an angel of the Lord appeared to Joseph in a dream. 'Get up,' he said, 'take the child and his mother and escape to Egypt. Stay there until I tell you, for Herod is going to search for the child to kill him.'

So he got up, took the child and his mother during the night and left for Egypt, where he stayed until the death of Herod. And so was fulfilled what the Lord had said through the prophet: 'Out of Egypt I called my son.'

When Herod realised that he had been outwitted by the Magi, he was furious, and he gave orders to kill all the boys in Bethlehem and its vicinity who were two years old and under, in accordance with the time he had learned from the Magi. Then what was said through the prophet Jeremiah was fulfilled:

> *'A voice is heard in Ramah,*
> *weeping and great mourning,*
> *Rachel weeping for her children*
> *and refusing to be comforted,*
> *because they are no more.'*

(Matthew 2:13 – 18)

Events in Bethlehem were, however, to take a turn for the worse once the Wise Men decided not to return home via Herod, having been warned of Herod s intentions in a dream. The king then exacted his wrath by massacring all the boys in Bethlehem under the age of two. Joseph and Mary, again forewarned in a dream, had fled for Egypt with Jesus.

The route they would have taken to escape is unknown, though from Bethlehem they would virtually have had to pass through Hebron, before the choice between two or more possible routes would have had to be made. Hebron is one of the most historic sites in Israel, the town in which Abraham, Isaac and Jacob stayed. After the original conquest of the land by Joshua it was made one of the six cities of refuge and assigned as a place of residence for the priesthood. Later it became the royal city of David for the first seven and a half years of his reign over Judah, and it was in Hebron that he was anointed king over all Israel. Less gloriously, it was from Hebron that Absalom launched his rebellion.

Hebron was also one of the cities fortified by Rehoboam and later rebuilt by the people of Israel upon their return from exile in Babylon. In the revolt against Rome it was captured and burnt before falling into relative obscurity until the time of the Crusaders. It was, however, remembered as the place of patriarchal burial, which may well explain its renewed importance to the Islamic world after the defeat of the Crusaders. Hebron since then has remained a devout Muslim town. In recent years it has been a major centre of Palestinian resistance and one of the first towns to obtain self-rule. David Roberts found Hebron to be a major Islamic centre in his day:

> *The population is about ten thousand Mahometans [Muslims], among whom are about 50 Jewish families . . . On turning the side of a hill, the little town of Hebron burst upon us. Its situation is beautiful; and the houses glittering in the noon-day sun had a look of English cleanliness, after the wretched hovels of Egypt. The children who came out to meet us, were among the most beautiful I had ever seen . . . As we went to show our passports at the house of the Deputy-Governor, we found many women weeping on the steps, and the Deputy engaged in the examination of a number of the unfortunate inhabitants who had been seized by the conscription. They were brought out in succession from a filthy-looking dungeon, and after inspection were handcuffed, and sent off.*

Hebron in 1839 appears dominated by its mosque. As usual David Roberts contrives to place an interesting human scene in the foreground.

Nazareth today is a closely-packed town spread over the surrounding hillside.

Chapter 4
Nazareth

Nazareth is the town in which Jesus grew up, and apart from the reference to that fact, the Gospels are silent concerning those years, as they are also about his adult life until his baptism. We simply read:

After Herod died, an angel of the Lord appeared in a dream to Joseph in Egypt and said, 'Get up, take the child and his mother and go to the land of Israel, for those who were trying to take the child's life are dead.'

So he got up, took the child and his mother and went to the land of Israel. But when he heard that Archelaus was reigning in Judea in place of his father Herod, he was afraid to go there. Having been warned in a dream, he withdrew to the district of Galilee, and he went and lived in a town called Nazareth. So was fulfilled what was said through the prophets: 'He will be called a Nazarene.'

(Matthew 2:19 – 25)

And the child grew and became strong; he was filled with wisdom, and the grace of God was upon him.

(Luke 2:40)

Roberts was impressed by the town of Nazareth, and waxed lyrical about the connection with the early life of our Lord:

The man must be insensible who can look on Nazareth without reverence for the might and mercy that once dwelt there. Generations pass away, and the noblest monuments of the hand of man follow them; but the hills, the valley, and the stream exist, on which the eye of the Lord all gazed; the soil on which His sacred footsteps trod; the magnificent landscape in the midst of which He lived.

Nazareth claims a number of holy sites, upon which since time immemorial various churches and shrines have been built. Possibly the most revered is the Fountain of the Virgin. As this was the only fountain in the town, it was held in great respect, not only as

A general view of Nazareth in 1846.

an important source of water, but in the belief that to this fountain Mary must constantly have come. The source is found under the Greek Church of the Assumption, some 50 yards to the north. The church is built over the source, at the spot where some claim the Virgin was visited by the angel Gabriel. From there, Roberts found the little stream was conducted by a small stone aqueduct, from the last arch of which it poured its waters into the so-called fountain — a sculptured marble trough, which may once have been a sarcophagus. He comments, concerning his illustration:

The figures introduced were all drawn on the spot, and convey an accurate representation of the female costume of Nazareth. Round the face, and hanging down on each side, they wear rows of gold and silver coins which, relieved by their jet-black locks, have a remarkably graceful and novel appearance to the European eye. The younger women were in general remarkably beautiful; and as they perceived in this instance that the strangers were Christians, they made no attempt to conceal their faces.

The Fountain of the Virgin, in 1839 (opposite) and the same site today, now incorporated into the Church of St Gabriel. The change in the last 160 years is dramatic.

Today, however, much is changed. The greatly enlarged church has been re-named. The fountain is no longer to be found outside, as David Roberts had observed, but the arch is still there, now situated in a side chapel of the Church of Gabriel.

Chapter 5

Jesus in the Temple

Concerning Jesus formative years, we simply read that: Every year his parents went to Jerusalem for the Feast of the Passover (Luke

Jerusalem from the north.
The pool and Roman columns in the foreground of
David Robert's sketch have disappeared: maybe they
were only artistic props.

2:41). As families in those days were close-knit and did most things together, and as travel in Roman-occupied Israel was safe, we can assume that Jesus would have visited Jerusalem annually with his family.

There can have been few sights as impressive as the first view of Jerusalem from the north — the route which the traveller from Galilee would most likely have taken. The view from this point is regarded as the most striking and extensive of Jerusalem. The

road, first descending into the valley of Jehoshaphat, crosses the ridge which extends between Mount Scopas and the Mount of Olives. The city is thus seen diagonally, and the view includes the Great Mosque and the deep valley, while, at the same time, the domes and minarets are seen with better effect than from the summit of Olivet.

The surrounding area has changed considerably in the past 150 years. Nonetheless, this first view of the holy city is extremely impressive, and never fails to move those seeing it for the first time. In Jesus day Herod s temple would have risen majestically, roughly where the Great Mosque now stands, and no pilgrim heading for Jerusalem would have failed to be moved by the sight. This is the setting for us to consider Jesus momentous visit to the temple at the age of twelve.

Every year his parents went to Jerusalem for the Feast of the Passover. When he was twelve years old, they went up to the Feast, according to the custom. After the Feast was

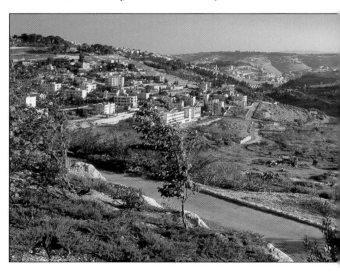

over, while his parents were returning home, the boy Jesus stayed behind in Jerusalem, but they were unaware of it. Thinking he was in their company, they travelled on for a day. Then they began looking for him among their relatives and friends. When they did not find him, they went back to Jerusalem to look for him. After three days they found him in the temple courts, sitting among the teachers, listening to them and asking them questions. Everyone who heard him was amazed at his understanding and his answers. When his parents saw him, they were astonished. His mother said to him, 'Son, why have you treated us like this? Your father and I have been anxiously searching for you.'

'Why were you searching for me?' he asked. 'Didn't you know I had to be in my Father's house?' But they did not understand what he was saying to them.

Then he went down to Nazareth with them and was obedient to them. But his mother treasured all these things in her heart. And Jesus grew in wisdom and stature, and in favour with God and men.

(Luke 2:41–52)

Jerusalem from the north, as seen from Mount Scopus today.

Chapter 6

The Baptism of Jesus

When David Roberts visited the Holy Land, the River Jordan flowed more strongly than today as its waters had not been diverted for irrigation. However, this wide sweep of the river with imposing cliffs in the background is difficult to reconcile with any specific riverbank location today.

While the baptism of Jesus marks the start of his ministry, and as such is of extreme importance, it must be said that, here again, it is impossible to precisely identify the location of the baptism. John obviously administered his baptism in the Jordan river. But over the centuries, the banks of the river have undoubtedly changed beyond recognition. They have further changed greatly since David Roberts day, as most of the water of the River Jordan has been diverted for irrigation. A mere trickle now flows at the traditional site of the baptism, further altering our perception today. A final difficulty is provided by the fact that the river is now the frontier between the states of Israel and Jordan, and access to the river at the traditionally claimed site of the baptism is prohibited for security reasons . . .

This extraordinary scene witnessed by David Roberts would today be impossible:

In this view Achmet Aga, the Governor of Jerusalem, with a part of his Arab guard, occupy the foreground. The River Jordan flows so deeply beneath its banks, that in crossing the plain from Jericho it is unseen. The stream runs about fifty feet below the level of the soil . . .

As we approached the brink of the River, a general rush took place, and the women broke into the shrill cry of joy so often heard in Egypt. Even the camels, though heavily loaded, could scarcely be restrained. The Governor s carpets were spread on a high bank close to the River, where we could command a view of the entire scene; the military band and colours were brought round him, and seats were assigned to our party.

One of the achievements is, to be the first to plunge into the stream; and on this occasion, a young Greek was swept away by the rapid current, and unfortunately drowned before our eyes. Young and old, male and female, were soon in the stream, some of them in imminent danger of being drowned. One of their superstitions is to put on slight dresses, which are to be preserved for their burial. This extra-ordinary display lasted about two hours, when the whole returned, the Governor now bringing up the rear.

The River Jordan at Delgany, the site currently associated with the baptism of Jesus.

Such a scene, with hundreds milling on the river bank and in the waters might have been more like the scenes of mass baptism during the height of John s ministry; as well as the scenes still common today — but in alternative sites — where pilgrims and worshippers congregate to be baptised in the waters of the Jordan. Jon Arnold s photograph captures the site of such modern-day baptisms, but in quieter, more reflective mood, as we read the biblical account:

Then Jesus came from Galilee to the Jordan to be baptised by John. But John tried to deter him, saying,

'I need to be baptised by you, and do you come to me?'

Jesus replied, 'Let it be so now; it is proper for us to do this to fulfil all righteousness.' Then John consented.

As soon as Jesus was baptised, he went up out of the water. At that moment heaven was opened, and he saw the Spirit of God descending like a dove and lighting on him. And a voice from heaven said, 'This is my Son, whom I love; with him I am well pleased.'

(Matthew 3:13–17)

The River Jordan at Delgany.

Chapter 7

The Temptation

Deep in the Judean Desert lies the Monastery of St Sabas or Mar Saba, at one stage a convent. Situated in the heart of the wilderness, on the edge of a precipice, the convent has been built on the site traditionally associated with Jesus temptation. Here again the exact location is debatable. Did Jesus even stay put for the full forty days during which he withdrew into the wilderness, or did he move around the Judean Desert? The Gospels are unclear, but whatever the exact location, few convey the harshness and aridity of the terrain as well as the Monastery of Mar Saba and its immediate surroundings.

> *It is impossible to imagine a more romantic or savage scene. The ravine cannot be less than five hundred feet in depth, perhaps more; the heights are wild. After a descent of three-quarters of an hour the fountain which gives name to the district is reached. The Ain-Jidy [the biblical Engedi] bursts forth at once a fine stream from a narrow shelf of the mountain, still more than four hundred feet above the level of the Dead Sea.*

In his journal David Roberts also describes the chapel and the convent, as he found them in 1840:

> *The Chapel in its general effect is beautiful; and the [Imperial] Russian government has signalised its care of the Greek churches in the East by adding to it some very striking ornaments. A short period before the date of this sketch, a number of pictures*

had been sent by the Imperial command, principally of saints, with the flesh painted, but the draperies and backgrounds in chased silver. The Convent, too, had undergone a thorough repair, as was presumed, from the same Imperial patronage.

A glimpse inside the monastery today.

No amount of fine devotional statuary and religious images will ever convey the enormity both of Jesus forty-day fast and the ensuing battle with the devil, and the victory which was to lay the foundations for and signal the start of Christ s ministry.

Jesus, full of the Holy Spirit, returned from the Jordan and was led by the Spirit in the desert, where for forty days he was tempted by the devil. He ate nothing during those days, and at the end of them he was hungry.

The devil said to him, 'If you are the Son of God, tell this stone to become bread.'

Jesus answered, 'It is written: "Man does not live on bread alone."'

The devil led him up to a high place and showed him in an instant all the kingdoms of the world. And he said to him, 'I will give you all their authority and splendour, for it has been given to me, and I can give it to anyone I want to. So if you worship me, it will all be yours.'

Jesus answered, 'It is written: "Worship the Lord your God and serve him only."'

The devil led him to Jerusalem and had him stand on the highest point of the temple. 'If you are the Son of God,' he said, 'throw yourself down from here. For it is written:

' "He will command his angels concerning you
to guard you carefully;
they will lift you up in their hands,
so that you will not strike your foot against
a stone."'

Jesus answered, 'It says: "Do not put the Lord your God to the test."'

When the devil had finished all this tempting, he left him until an opportune time.

(Luke 4:1–13)

(Previous pages:) The monastery of Mar Saba, in 1839 and today.
(Above): Mar Saba, perched on the edge of a precipice is both striking and well-preserved.

Chapter 8

Jesus Calls His
Disciples

We now move to Galilee, the principal area of Jesus ministry, and to the calling of the first disciples. As Matthew s Gospel says:

As Jesus was walking beside the Sea of Galilee, he saw two brothers, Simon called Peter and his brother Andrew. They were casting a net into the lake, for they were fishermen. 'Come, follow me,' Jesus said, 'and I will make you fishers of men.' At once they left their nets and followed him.

Going on from there, he saw two other brothers, James son of Zebedee and his brother John. They were in a boat with their father Zebedee, preparing their nets. Jesus called them, and immediately they left the boat and their father and followed him.

(Matthew 4:18 – 22)

This is one of the sites which, as many in the region, changed little between Jesus day and David Roberts visit, other than a general decay and abandonment of the substantial Roman buildings, and the baths in particular. David Roberts took the columns in the foreground to mark the site of ancient public baths. Tiberias possesses a hot water spring from which sulphurous water issues at about 144° Fahrenheit. He visited the baths, which had been rebuilt a hundred yards from the original site:

The town of Tiberias has grown considerably, although the old fortress is still visible in the centre of the picture.

This bath was crowded with pilgrims, who at this season were returning from Jerusalem. Above the bathing house is a large reservoir, into which the water is first received, and allowed to cool before it flows into the bath . . .

The view of Tiberias and the Lake from this spot, backed as it is by the snowy summits of Lebanon, is strikingly picturesque; but it wants wood, though the vegetation is rank in grass, brambles and low shrubs.

Chapter 9

The First Miracle

Having selected his first disciples, Jesus performs the first miracle, perhaps somewhat reluctantly, and certainly it is one which differs from the various healings we encounter throughout the Gospels. Nonetheless, it undoubtedly

revealed his glory and his power over the natural world, confirmed his special calling and enabled his newly-chosen disciples to put their faith in him.

On the third day a wedding took place at Cana in Galilee. Jesus' mother was there, and Jesus and his disciples had also been invited to the wedding. When the wine was gone, Jesus' mother said to him, 'They have no more wine.'

'Dear woman, why do you involve me?' Jesus replied, 'My time has not yet come.'

His mother said to the servants, 'Do whatever he tells you.'

The hills around Cana and the village itself have changed little over the years. David Roberts was, however, tempted to turn the rolling hills in the foreground into something a little more dramatic!

Nearby stood six stone water jars, the kind used by the Jews for ceremonial washing, each holding from twenty to thirty gallons.

Jesus said to the servants, 'Fill the jars with water'; so they filled them to the brim.

Then he told them, 'Now draw some out and take it to the master of the banquet.'

They did so, and the master of the banquet tasted the water that had been turned into wine. He did not realise

where it had come from, though the servants who had drawn the water knew. Then he called the bridegroom aside and said, 'Everyone brings out the choice wine first and then the cheaper wine after the guests have had too much to drink; but you have saved the best till now.'

This, the first of his miraculous signs, Jesus performed at Cana in Galilee. He thus revealed his glory, and his disciples put their faith in him.

(John 2:1–11)

In the watercolour on the previous page David
Roberts chose to focus on a broader view of the
countryside surrounding the small village of Cana,
rather than any of the details he found within the
village, as he states:

> *In the small Greek Church at the foot of the hill,*
> *is shown by the priest, as an invaluable relic (on the*

*David Roberts has also left us this delicate sketch of
the well at Cana, from which the water used for the
miracle is supposed to have been drawn.*

*Inset opposite page: Storage jars, such as these, were
in use in Palestine in the first century.*

*authority of tradition), one of the water pots in which the water was changed into wine. For preservation, it is built into the wall. The Church itself is pronounced to have been raised on the spot where the marriage - feast was celebrated. The ruins of an adjacent house are regarded, on the same authority, **to be those of those dwelling of our** Lord: the disciple Nathanael was reputed to be a native of Cana.*

Chapter 10

The Beatitudes

The view from the hill above Nazareth, writes David Roberts, *is one of the most striking in Palestine. Beneath it lies the chief part of the Plain of Esdraelon. To the left is seen the summit of Mount Tabor, over intervening hills; with portions of the Little Hermon, Gilboa, and the opposite mountains*

of Samaria. The long line of Carmel is visible, stretching to the sea. In the West spreads the Mediterranean, always lovely, and reflecting every colour of the morning and evening sky. On the North opens out a verdant and beautiful plain, now called El-Buttauf. Beyond this plain, long ridges of hills, extending East and West, are overtopped by the mountains of Safed, crowned with that city. Towards the right is a sea of hills and mountains, backed by the still higher ridge beyond the Lake of Tiberias, and on the N.E. by Mount Hermon with its icy crown.

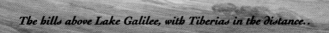

The hills above Lake Galilee, with Tiberias in the distance..

73

This is the glorious site Jesus chose to retire to a number of times, and it is also on one of these hills overlooking the lake that Jesus chose to feed the five thousand, and to use as his backdrop for the beatitudes.

Now when [Jesus] saw the crowds, he went up on a mountainside and sat down. His disciples came to him, and he began to teach them, saying:

'Blessed are the poor in spirit,
 for theirs is the kingdom of heaven.
Blessed are those who mourn,
 for they will be comforted.
Blessed are the meek,
 for they will inherit the earth.
Blessed are those who hunger and thirst after

righteousness,
  for they will be filled.
Blessed are the merciful,
  for they will be shown mercy.
Blessed are the pure in heart,
  for they will see God.
Blessed are the peacemakers,
  for they will be called sons of God.
Blessed are those who are persecuted
    because of righteousness,
  for theirs is the kingdom of heaven.
  Blessed are you when people insult you, persecute you and falsely say all kinds of evil against you because of me. Rejoice and be glad, because great is your reward in heaven, for in the same way they persecuted the prophets who were before you.'

(Matthew 5:1–12)

The hills above Tiberias today, with the Sea of Galilee and the Golan Heights in the distance. Many of the hillsides have been terraced centuries ago for the cultivation of olives, wheat and vines.

Chapter 11

The Pool of Bethesda

Now there is in Jerusalem near the Sheep Gate a pool, which in Aramaic is called Bethesda and which is surrounded by five covered colonnades. Here a great number of disabled people used to lie – the blind, the lame, the paralysed. One who was there had been an invalid for

thirty-eight years. When Jesus saw him lying there and learned that he had been in this condition for a long time, he asked him, 'Do you want to get well?'

'Sir,' the invalid replied, 'I have no-one to help me into the pool when the water is stirred. While I am trying to get in, someone else goes down ahead of me.'

Then Jesus said to him, 'Get up! Pick up your mat and walk.' At once the man was cured; he picked up his

mat and walked.

The day on which this took place was a Sabbath, and so the Jews said to the man who had been healed, 'It is the Sabbath; the law forbids you to carry your mat.'

But he replied, 'The man who made me well said to me, "Pick up your mat and walk." '

(John 5:2–11)

The Pool of Bethesda, from a similar angle to David Roberts vantage point.

Since the earliest documented times, this former reservoir to the north of the Temple Mount has been known as the Pool of Bethesda. In the opinion of many, however, this may not have been the actual site of the pool where Jesus healed the man who had been an invalid for thirty-eight years. The biblical pool was situated near the Sheep Gate and would presumably have been used to wash the sheep before they were taken into the temple for sacrifice.

The Pool of Bethesda today with the church of St Anne.

The pool featured here measures some 360 by 130 feet and is still about 75 feet deep, though a great deal of earth and debris lies in it. It is more of a reservoir than a pool.

The bottom is currently always dry, though at the time of David Roberts visit in April 1840, it contained some stagnant water, as well as a few shrubs and trees, as can be seen from his illustration, featured overleaf.

The view, David Roberts informs us, *is taken from the street leading to the Great Mosque. The characteristic feature of Jewish architecture is exhibited in the domes, which form the roof of every house, a result of the costliness of timber; but, from its wanting the lightness of the Oriental dome, in general the effect is poor and monotonous. The tower on the right is the minaret standing in the enclosure of the mosque, and the ruins beneath are conceived to be the remnants of the Tower of Antonia.*

The site of the pool of Bethesda is today virtually unrecognisable: archaeology is a growth business in modern-day Israel, and it would appear that nowhere has been as much excavated as this site! Layer upon layer has been peeled away and both Jon Arnold s photos provide a fair idea — from two different angles — of the depth of the pool, as well as the constricted nature of the site. It is hardly surprising that the cripple mentioned in the Gospel needed help to reach the waters.

It is also to be noted that the many minarets of nearby mosques which feature so prominently in David Roberts painting are today nowhere to be seen, and one of them most certainly appears to have been replaced by a church. This is the unprepossessing site for one of Jesus most remarkable miracles.

Chapter 12

Jesus is Rejected
at Nazareth

In his diary Roberts gives us a few factual details about the town and its inhabitants, which he visited in 1840.

The town of Nazareth lies on the western side of a narrow, oblong basin. The houses stand on the lower slope of the western hill, which rises steep and

high above them: the dwellings are in general well built, and of stone; they have flat, terraced roofs, without the domes so common in Southern Palestine. The population is about three thousand souls, of which the Mahometans compose 120 families; the rest are Greek, Latin and Maronite [Christians].

(Jesus) went to Nazareth, where he had been brought up, and on the Sabbath day he went into the synagogue, as was his custom. And he stood up to read. The scroll of the prophet Isaiah was handed to him. Unrolling it, he found the place where it is written:

'The Spirit of the Lord is on me,
  because he has anointed me
  to preach good news to the poor.
He has sent me to proclaim freedom for the
  prisoners
  and recovery of sight for the blind,
to release the oppressed,
  to proclaim the year of the Lord's favour.'

*Today Nazareth is a large thriving town of well over 100,000
people and has grown virtually beyond recognition. Only the
hills beyond appear unchanged in the photograph taken from
the same vantage point as David Roberts' watercolour.*

Then he rolled up the scroll, gave it back to the attendant and sat down. The eyes of everyone in the synagogue were fastened on him, and he began by saying to them, 'Today this scripture is fulfilled in your hearing.'

All spoke well of him and were amazed at the gracious words that came from his lips. 'Isn't this Joseph's son?' they asked.

Jesus said to them, 'Surely you will quote this proverb to me: "Physician, heal yourself! Do here in your home town what we have heard that you did in Capernaum."'

'I tell you the truth,' he continued, 'no prophet is accepted in his home town. I assure you that there were many widows in Israel in Elijah's time, when the sky was

Though we do not know where the precipice was from which the townsfolk intended to plunge Jesus to his death, a number of outcrops near the town might have provided the location.

shut for three and a half years and there was a severe famine throughout the land. Yet Elijah was not sent to any of them, but to a widow in Zarephath in the region of Sidon. And there were many in Israel with leprosy in the time of Elisha the prophet, yet not one of them was cleansed – only Naaman the Syrian.'

All the people in the synagogue were furious when they heard this. They got up, drove him out of the town, and took him to the brow of the hill on which the town was built, in order to throw him down the cliff. But he walked right through the crowd and went on his way.

(Luke 4:16–30)

Chapter 13

Jesus Feeds the Five Thousand

Somewhere on the hills above the lake, in a quiet spot, lies the site of the feeding of the five thousand, far away from the hustle of the thriving lakeside towns.

When Jesus looked up and saw a great crowd coming towards him, he said to Philip, 'Where shall we buy bread

for these people to eat?' He asked this only to test him, for he already had in mind what he was going to do.

Philip answered him, 'Eight months' wages would not buy enough bread for each one to have a bite!'

Another of his disciples, Andrew, Simon Peter's brother, spoke up, 'Here is a boy with five small barley loaves and two small fish, but how far will they go among so many?'

Jesus said, 'Make the people sit down.' There was plenty of grass in that place, and the men sat down, about five thousand of them. Jesus then took the loaves, gave thanks, and distributed to those who were seated as much as they wanted. He did the same with the fish.

Above and opposite: The modern town of Tiberias, seen from the suburb of Hammat.

When they had all had enough to eat, he said to his disciples, 'Gather the pieces that are left over. Let nothing be wasted.' So they gathered them and filled twelve baskets with the pieces of the five barley loaves left over by those who had eaten.

After the people saw the miraculous sign that Jesus did, they began to say, 'Surely this is the Prophet who is to come into the world.' Jesus, knowing that they intended to come and make him king by force, withdrew again to a mountain by himself.

(John 6:5–15)

Chapter 14

Jesus Calms the Storm

Passing through a beautiful country, in about five hours we came in sight of the Sea of Galilee,

*embosomed in surrounding hills; far on the left lay
Mount Hermon, covered with snow; and on a
nearer hill rests the city of Safed. Here, at a glance,
lay before us the scenes of our Saviour's miracles; but
the population and the boats have disappeared.
Towards the west the River Jordan was seen flowing
from the lake towards the Dead Sea, and below us
lay the town of Tiberias . . . The lake presents,*

*indeed, a beautiful sheet of limpid water, in a deep,
depressed basin. The hills are rounded and tame,
with little of picturesque in their form; they are
decked by no shrubs or forests, and even the verdure
of the grass, which earlier in the season might have
given them a pleasing aspect, was already gone; they
were now only naked and dreary. One interesting
object greeted our eyes, — a little boat with a white
sail, gliding over the waters: the only one, as we
afterwards found, upon the lake.*

Times have changed since David Roberts visit:
today there are many boats on the lake; the population has greatly increased; but most noticeably, the
surrounding land is intensively cultivated. Fields,
forests, groves and plentiful irrigation have trans-
formed the landscape.

*The Sea of Tiberias, looking towards the Golan, today
and on previous pages in 1840.*

Storms still rise frequently and unexpectedly, as strong and sudden winds blow in gustily and fiercely from the Syrian desert. What was a few moments before a quiet and placid lake, can quickly become a windswept, heaving surface of treacherous water.

Then he got into the boat and his disciples followed him. Without warning, a furious storm came up on the lake, so that the waves swept over the boat. But Jesus was sleeping. The disciples went and woke him, saying, 'Lord, save us! We're going to drown!'

He replied, 'You of little faith, why are you so afraid?' Then he got up and rebuked the winds and the waves, and it was completely calm.

The men were amazed and asked, 'What kind of man is this? Even the winds and the waves obey him!'

(Matthew 8:23–27)

Chapter 15
The Narrow Door

The Damascus Gate is today a busy focal point in Jerusalem. Well preserved, it has itself hardly changed through the centuries, except that its approach has been made more even and is now a busy square.

Jerusalem has four open gates and four walled up. Of the four open gates, facing the four points of the compass, that of which the view is given looks to the north, and is called by the natives Bab-el-Hamud, or the Gate of the Pillar. The Damascus Gate is a name given by the Europeans, from its leading to Damascus and Nabulus by the great northern road. It is more ornamented than the others, and forms a striking object to the traveller.

As David Roberts noted it is one of Jerusalem s original eight gates, and is certainly the best preserved today. It is typical of an old city gate, narrow and foreboding, difficult of access. Did Jesus have such a door in mind when he told the following parable ?

Then Jesus went through the towns and villages, teaching as he made his way to Jerusalem. Someone asked him, 'Lord, are only a few people going to be saved?'

He said to them, 'Make every effort to enter through the narrow door, because many, I tell you, will try to enter and will not be able to. Once the owner of the house gets up and closes the door, you will stand outside knocking and pleading, "Sir, open the door for us." . . .

'There will be weeping there, and gnashing of teeth, when you see Abraham, Isaac and Jacob and all the prophets in the kingdom of God, but you yourselves thrown out. People will come from east and west and north and south, and will take their places at the feast in the kingdom of God. Indeed there are those who are last who will be first, and first who will be last.'

(Luke 13:22–30)

Chapter 16

Jesus Heals the Man Born Blind

The Kidron valley and the area around the Pool of Siloam in David Roberts' day.

103

The Pool of Siloam is well documented through the miracle of the healing of the man born blind. The identification of its location, outside the city walls in the valley of Jehoshaphat, goes back to the earliest times, though the pool itself has undergone numerous changes. It is currently a small, rectangular, deeply-sunk pool, surrounded by houses. Jerome, in the fourth century, describes it as a fountain at the foot of mount Sion, whose waters do not flow regularly . In AD 1185 a certain Phocas states it to be surrounded by arches and massive columns, with gardens below .

In Roberts time, it would appear that all superstructures had been demolished or fallen into ruin, and that the pool was but a small reservoir, on the side of the hill.

Above & opposite: The Pool of Siloam today.

The ridge ends here, just over the Pool of Siloam, in a steep point of rock. Along its base the water is conducted from the pool in a small channel hewn in the rock, and led off, to water the gardens of fig and other fruit-trees lying in terraces, which extend to the bottom of the Valley of Jehoshaphat, a descent of forty or fifty feet. Siloam is now used as a public fountain.

Today, the immediate surrounds have been densely built up, though, as the photograph indicates, the overall area has changed little. Siloam is now Silwan, a predominantly Arab neighbourhood. This is the site for the following event.

As he went along, he saw a man blind from birth. His disciples asked him, 'Rabbi, who sinned, this man or his parents, that he was born blind?'

'Neither this man nor his parents sinned,' said Jesus, 'but this happened so that the work of God might be displayed in his life. As long as it is day, we must do the work of him who sent me. Night is coming, when no-one can work. While I am in the world, I am the light of the world.'

Having said this, he spat on the ground, made some mud with the saliva, and put it on the man's eyes. 'Go,' he

told him, 'wash in the Pool of Siloam' (this word means Sent). So the man went and washed, and came home seeing.

His neighbours and those who had formerly seen him begging asked, 'Isn't this the same man who used to sit and beg?' Some claimed that he was.

Others said, 'No, he only looks like him.'

But he himself insisted, 'I am the man.'

'How then were your eyes opened?' they demanded.

He replied, 'The man they call Jesus made some mud and put it on my eyes. He told me to go to Siloam and wash. So I went and washed, and then I could see.'

'Where is this man?' they asked him.

'I don't know,' he said.

(John 9:1–12)

Near the Pool of Siloam: the Arab neighbourhood of Silwan.

Chapter 17

The Good Samaritan

On many occasions Jesus and his disciples travelled between Jerusalem and Jericho. They would very likely have taken the most direct — and well-travelled — route once they left behind them the villages surrounding the capital.

Very quickly they would have witnessed a dramatic change in scenery, as little villages and well-cultivated hillsides gave place to the arid, seemingly

never-ending stretches of the Judean Desert. Though well frequented, the road was renowned as the favoured haunt of marauding robbers, who would swoop down on the unsuspecting traveller, attack and make off with their bounty, to disappear just as quickly into the ravines that puncture the landscape.

This is the setting Jesus chose as backdrop for one of his most memorable parables: the story of the Good Samaritan.

On one occasion an expert in the law stood up to test Jesus. 'Teacher' he asked, 'what must I do to inherit eternal life?'

The valley of the Jordan and the Dead Sea.

The Oasis of Jericho seen from the final barren hills of the Judean Desert.

'What is written in the Law?' he replied. 'How do you read it?'

He answered: ' "Love the Lord your God with all your heart and with all your soul and with all your strength and with all your mind"; and, "Love your neighbour as yourself." '

'You have answered correctly,' Jesus replied. 'Do this and you will live.'

But he wanted to justify himself, so he asked Jesus, 'And who is my neighbour?'

In reply Jesus said: 'A man was going down from Jerusalem to Jericho, when he fell into the hands of

robbers. They stripped him of his clothes, beat him and went away, leaving him half-dead. A priest happened to be going down the same road, and when he saw the man, he passed by on the other side. So too, a Levite, when he came to the place and saw him, passed by on the other side. But a Samaritan, as he travelled, came where the man was; and when he saw him, he took pity on him. He went to him and bandaged his wounds, pouring on oil and wine. Then he put the man on his own donkey, brought him to an inn and took care of him. The next day he took out two silver coins and gave them to the innkeeper. "Look after him," he said, "and when I return, I will reimburse you for any extra expense you may have."

'Which of these three do you think was a neighbour to the man who fell into the hands of the robbers?'

The expert in the law replied, 'The one who had mercy on him.'

Jesus told him, 'Go and do likewise'

(Luke 10:25–37)

The view, says David Roberts, was one not to be forgotten. The Valley of the Jordan lay stretched beneath our feet, in all the beauty of an Eastern evening. The Dead Sea, the silvery line of the rapid Jordan just visible, the gay colours of the pilgrim encampment glittering in the last rays of the setting

sun, were fitter for the poet than the painter. The pencil must fail to realise it. On the whole line of road were Arab and Bedouin lancers.

Many travellers throughout the centuries have described the terrain and the splendid vistas stretching seemingly to infinity. Such atmospheric clarity is uncommon today, due to pollution. However, Jon Arnold s photograph captures the scene, from just outside Jerusalem, on an exceptionally clear autumn day. The hills in the far distance, beyond the Dead Sea (hidden in the valley) are over 60 miles (100 kilometres) away.

Chapter 18

The Transfiguration

Jesus . . . took Peter, John and James with him and went up onto a mountain to pray. As he was praying, the appearance of his face changed, and his clothes became as bright as a flash of lightning. Two men, Moses and

Mount Tabor from the Plain of Esdraelon.

Elijah, appeared in glorious splendour, talking with Jesus. They spoke about his departure, which he was about to bring to fulfilment at Jerusalem. Peter and his companions were very sleepy, but when they became fully awake, they saw his glory and the two men standing with him. As the men were leaving Jesus, Peter said to him, 'Master, it is good for us to be here. Let us put up three shelters — one for you, one for Moses and one for Elijah.' (He did not know what he was saying.)

115

Mount Tabor

While he was speaking, a cloud appeared and enveloped them, and they were afraid as they entered the cloud. A voice came from the cloud, saying, 'This is my Son, whom I have chosen; listen to him.' When the voice had spoken, they found that Jesus was alone. The disciples kept this to themselves, and told no-one at that time what they had seen.

(Luke 9:28–36)

The present view of Mount Tabor, observed David Roberts, *was taken while crossing the plain, on the road from Jenin to Nazareth. It is the very opposite of the ruggedness and grandeur given to its form in the sketches I had hitherto seen. Though a fine hill, it has long lost all claims to the picturesque; the labours of the ancient population having cleared and shaped it into its present form. In many instances this process may be still traced by the terraces remaining on the sides, though often, by time, indistinguishable in colour from the rocks on which they are raised. The general character of the hills of Palestine is roundness, arising from the same cause.*

The view from Mount Tabor

Chapter 19

The Triumphal Entry into Jerusalem

A procession in Jaffa, in the late nineteenth century

Processions which might in any way capture the sheer vitality and joy of Jesus triumphal entry are impossible to replicate. Every procession will seem somewhat flat by comparison to the Gospel account.

This illustration, by a contemporary of David Roberts who visited Jerusalem a few years later than him, captures just such a procession making its way through the crowded streets some 150 years ago. Is it a wedding; a civic event, or some other celebration? We will never know, but the image the artist has left us does convey in a pale replica, some of the hustle and joyous anticipation of Jesus progress through the narrow, crowded streets.

As they approached Jerusalem and came to Bethphage on the Mount of Olives, Jesus sent two disciples, saying to them, 'Go to the village ahead of you, and at once you will find a donkey tied there, with her colt by her. Untie them and bring them to me. If anyone says anything to you, tell him that the Lord needs them, and he will send them right away.'

This took place to fulfil what was spoken through the prophet:

'Say to the Daughter of Zion,
"See, your king comes to you,
gentle and riding on a donkey,
on a colt, the foal of a donkey"'

The disciples went and did as Jesus had instructed them. They brought the donkey and the colt, placed their cloaks on them, and Jesus sat on them. A very large crowd spread their cloaks on the road, while others cut branches from the trees and spread them on the road. The crowds that went ahead of him and those that followed shouted,

Hosanna to the Son of David!'

'Blessed is he who comes in the name of the Lord!'

'Hosanna in the highest!'

When Jesus entered Jerusalem, the whole city was stirred and asked, 'Who is this?'

The crowds answered, 'This is Jesus, the prophet from Nazareth in Galilee.'

Matthew 21:1–11

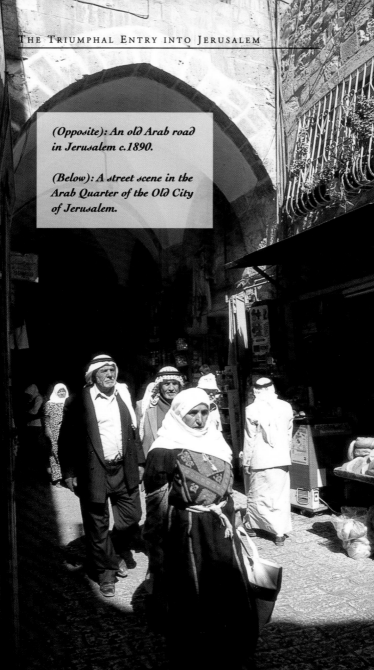

(Opposite): An old Arab road in Jerusalem c.1890.

(Below): A street scene in the Arab Quarter of the Old City of Jerusalem.

Chapter 20

Jesus Weeps
Over Jerusalem

Then Jesus said to the crowds and to his disciples . . .
'O Jerusalem, Jerusalem, you who kill the prophets

and stone those sent to you, how often I have longed to gather your children together, as a hen gathers her chicks under her wings, but you were not willing. Look, your house is left to you desolate. For I tell you, you will not see me again until you say, "Blessed is he who comes in the name of the Lord".'

Matthew 23:37–39

Roberts provides some useful commentary in his journal to accompany this particular painting:

> Jerusalem lies near the summit of a broad mountain ridge. The breadth of the whole site of the town from the Valley of Hinnom to the Valley of Jehoshaphat is just over 1000 yards. The surrounding country is of limestone formation. The region is dreary, and the soil seems sterile; yet the olive thrives, and corn is grown in the levels and valleys. The vine and fig-tree flourish no longer on the hills, but the later grows in sheltered spots and is frequent near Bethlehem.
>
> The spectator is presumed to be standing on the Mount of Olives, looking towards the Mosque of Omar, which stands on the central point of the view. On its left is the Mosque El Aska. The space within which those edifices stand, is enclosed by a wall of great thickness, formed of stones of remarkable size, some of them thirty feet, and with a great probability supposed to have formed part of the original wall of the platform, on which stood the temple built by

Herod. Beyond, and rising above it, is Mount Sion, the site of the city of David.

At the foot of the spectator is the valley of Jehoshaphat, through which flows the brook Kedron. Immediately under the Gate of St Stephen is a small church traditionally standing over the burial place of the Virgin Mary. Close to it is the memorable Garden of Gethsamene. To the right of the garden, and lower down are the disputed pools of Siloam.

Roberts journal concludes with an interesting entry concerning Jerusalem in his day, and still very much the prayer of many today.and which we hope this small book will have opened the eyes of your mind and your heart to:

The eyes of Europe have been directed to it in our day, with an interest unfelt since the age of the Crusades, and founded on higher principles than those of worldly ambition. At this hour, the whole Christian world, by a new and nobler impulse, prays for the peace of Jerusalem .

Picture Credits

All photographs are by Jon Arnold and used with kind permission.

All other art illustrations are credited as follows:

1	Olive Grove, North Israel
2-3	*Prayers near the Pool of Bethesda*, David Roberts, 1839—40.
4-5	*Ancient Jaffa*, David Roberts, 1839—40
6-7	Sunrise over Galilee
8-9	Bedouin leading camel in the desert (The Image Bank)
10	*The Walls of Jerusalem*, Carl Werner, c. 1880.
14-15	Detail from *A view across the Kidron Valley to the Temple Mount*, David Roberts, 1839—40.
17	*Jerusalem with the flooded Pool of Bethesda in the foreground,* Nathaniel Green, c. 1860.
22	*A general view of Nazareth*, Van de Velde, 1851
24-25	*The Interior of the Church of the Annunciation,* David Roberts, 1839—40.
28-29	*General view of Bethlehem,* David Roberts, 1839—40.
38-39	*Hebron in 1839,* David Roberts, 1839.
42-43	*Nazareth — a general view,* David Roberts, 1839—40.
44	*The Fountain of the Virgin,* David Roberts, 1839—40.